Being
Sara

Being Sara.
COPYRIGHT 2009
by Christopher Passudetti

Scobre Press Corporation
2255 Calle Clara
La Jolla, CA 92307

First Scobre edition published 2009.
Edited by Ramey Temple
Cover Design by Michael Lynch

ISBN (10) # 1-934713-91-0
ISBN (13) # 978-1-934713-91-4

HOME RUN EDITION

This story is based on the life of Sara-Elizabeth Clark,
although some names, quotes, and details of events
have been altered.

Chapter One

Red Carpet Dreams

It's Oscar Night and there's excitement in the air. All of Hollywood's biggest stars have come out. Wearing expensive designer clothing, they step out of stretch limousines. Hanging around their necks are diamonds, sapphires, emeralds and pearls as big as olives. Smiling for photographs and looking fabulous, they walk the red carpet with confidence.

Nearly one billion people around the world are watching these events unfold on live television. From New York to Paris, the best of show business is on display.

1

Back at her Malibu beach house, Sara takes one last look at herself in the mirror. She admires the fancy dress she had custom-made for tonight. Meanwhile, her makeup artist applies the finishing touches to her face. Her friends probably wouldn't recognize her all made up. That's because she normally wears a pair of comfy blue pajama pants.

In this daydream, Sara's home is the fourth from the right. If you look really closely, you can see her makeup artist applying some last-minute eye shadow.

Sara says a quick goodbye to Jessica, her three-foot-long pet iguana. Then she steps out the door and into a zebra-striped Hummer limousine. It's only the best for the most promising newcomer Hollywood has seen in years.

On the way to the Oscars, a Young Jeezy song plays loudly on the stereo. Sara sticks her head out of the Hummer's oversized moonroof and feels the wind whip through her hair. Cruising down Ventura Boulevard, she takes it all in.

The Hummer, with its tinted windows, comes rolling up to the theater. Sara ducks back inside, grabbing her handheld mirror and taking one last look at herself. "Looking good," she whispers. "I am ready to go."

Taking a deep breath as the car slows, Sara is ready to make her grand entrance. Her driver opens the door slowly. The flood of noise breaks through and rushes into

the car. Sara steps out onto the red carpet and suddenly it all becomes very real.

The paparazzi turn their attention to Sara. They gather around her with flashbulbs snapping. Being a star feels exactly the way Sara had always imagined it would.

"Sara, look over here!"

"Who are you wearing tonight, Sara?"

"Just one more shot before you head in!"

"Do you think you're going to win?"

Sara's mind begins to wander as she passes through the crowd. What if I do win? she wonders. The possibilities are endless!

In the midst of these thoughts, the flashbulbs get brighter until Sara can't see anything. The lights surround *her. She hears her name being called out. "Sara...Sara...*

Sara-Elizabeth.... You're dreaming, Sara...Wake up!"

Sara awoke to find herself in the middle of a long line. She had let herself drift off, ending up in a familiar red carpet daydream. Her father was tapping her on the arm. "Sara," he whispered. "Hello?"

"I'm here," she said dreamily. "I just forgot where we were for a minute."

Looking down at the script in her hands, it all came

rushing back to her. She and her father had taken a trip to New York City that morning for her very first movie audition.

Sara observed all of the competition that surrounded her. There were literally hundreds of girls gathered in that line. They were all different sizes, shapes and ages. But they were all driven by the same dream: to be a star on the big screen.

In April of 2007, the magazine *American Girl* had advertised an open casting call in several major cities. The magazine was casting for a new mystery movie. It was based on one of the magazine's characters, Kit Kittredge. They were looking to fill the role of Kit's best friend. And they had sent the word out for girls to come out and give it a shot.

The chance to be in a movie with Abigail Breslin—the young actress who starred in *Little Miss Sunshine*—was too big to pass up. Sara got permission to miss a day of school and headed south to New York City. It was about ninety miles from her home in the town of New Paltz, New York. She just had to take her shot at making that red carpet dream a reality.

Above, Sara lounges on a rock wall in her hometown of New Paltz, New York.

Not surprisingly, a "few" other people had the same idea. When Sara and her father had shown up in Manhattan, they were greeted by a line that poured out of the *American*

Girl headquarters. The line went around an entire city block. Over a thousand people had shown up to audition for a single part! The scene was electric and the competition was intense.

Just in case you have never seen one, a line of a thousand teenage girls is a sight. There were cell phones ringing every couple of seconds, and constant laughter. There was more text messaging, *US Weekly*-reading, and lip gloss-applying than you could possibly imagine. Most importantly, this line of teens moved very, *very* slowly.

Thirty-five games of *Twenty Questions* later, Sara and her dad felt as if they hadn't moved very far. At one point, they had to look around to make sure the line hadn't begun moving backward.

The line crept along like that for three hours. But as they turned the last corner of the city block, they could finally see the entrance to *American Girl*. The building was as beautiful as they had heard it was.

As soon as they stepped into the building, a staff member took a whole group of girls aside. She explained to them what to expect in the first audition. "We'll call you into the auditorium. You'll line up on stage with your toes on the blue tape. We'll go down the line and ask each of you who you are. Then we'll have you read the lines you've prepared for us," she said looking out at the girls. "This is the process for the first audition. If you make it through to the next one, we'll give you a number and ask you to stick around. Good luck, ladies."

Sara's heart started to beat a little faster. It wasn't out of nervousness, but out of sheer excitement. About five minutes later, the auditorium door flew open and Sara's group was called inside. Sara grabbed her script and headed through the doorway. She found the blue-tape line and put her toes on the edge of it. The rest of her group found their spots and the audition began.

"Tell us who you are. Then go ahead and read the lines from the script you brought," a woman called out from the auditorium seats. Two men were sitting beside her, holding notebooks and looking very serious.

The first girl in line began, "My name is Denise Thomas. Should I just read my..." she cleared her throat and then began to read her lines: "Mother, I'm going to Kit's house with Francis..."

Two more girls followed right after her. One did really well, and the other one pretty much freaked out. The girls seemed either really nervous or super confident. One forgot her lines and left the room without saying a word. The sixth girl in line had a different problem altogether: "My name is…uh…uh…wait, can I start over?"

Sara was next. She looked straight at the judges with a smile. "My name is Sara-Elizabeth," she began, and then delivered her lines in a confident voice. "Don't worry, Ruthie. Bad guys always get caught in the end." She nailed it.

After the last three girls went, Sara headed for the exit with the rest of her group. She had one foot out the door when she was pulled aside and handed a piece of paper. Sara turned it over and saw the number 116 printed on the other side. "We'd like to invite you to a second reading, so stick around and we'll call your number a little later." Sara, holding the piece of paper tightly, smiled brightly.

Sara rushed out of the auditorium door. She ran over to her dad and hugged him. Clutching her number tightly, she wasted no time getting out her script. She wanted to prepare for the second round of auditions.

The problem was that she was too excited to focus on the script. While beginning to daydream again, her script dropped to the floor. She leaned forward to pick it up. The one short leg of her wobbly chair caught her eye. A crooked line of initials made its way down the chair's leg.

Sara reached into her pocket and pulled out her key chain. She was thinking about all the other girls who had sat in this chair before their auditions and left their initials behind. Sara decided to do the same. She grabbed her house key and carefully etched the initials "S.C." into the wooden leg. Her dad leaned over and asked, "What are you doing, Sara?"

"I'm making history," she said. "This is a great moment. I want to remember it—and be remembered."

Sara had had a childhood filled with uncertainty, and had dealt with a serious medical condition. Because of this, she had learned to appreciate life's great moments. For much of her life, she had not thought an experience like this would have been possible. As she stared down at her initials, Sara began to realize that she had become part of something special just by showing up at that audition. Getting invited to the second reading was the icing on the cake.

Chapter Two

Mixed Signals

"Hi, my name is Sara-Elizabeth Clark. I have epilepsy. But I am currently seizure free and off all medications." This is how Sara introduces herself on her website www.itsnotwhoiam.com.

The definition of a seizure is a period of unusual movement or behavior resulting from abnormal electrical activity in the brain. Seizures can make a person lose consciousness and even shake uncontrollably. You'd never know it by looking at Sara, but there was a time in her life when the threat of a seizure coming on at any moment was a very frightening possibility.

Currently fourteen years old, Sara is seizure free and very excited about the progress she has made with acting. She hopes to one day make her red carpet dreams come true. Making it past the first cut at the *American Girl* movie audition was a positive step.

For awhile, Sara's own life story was kind of like a movie. She describes it as a thriller movie—and like any good thriller, her life started out very normal. Sara spent the first year of her life eating, sleeping and crying. It was a pretty quiet first year.

Sara and her two sisters, Machele and Kymmie, were playing together one summer afternoon in 1996 when their mother turned around at just the wrong moment. Looking back as the sound of the girls playing hushed for a second, she watched Sara's eyes roll back in her head. She looked on in horror as Sara slumped backward. Only sixteen months old, Sara was unresponsive for several seconds. When she awoke, she was crying a little, but seemed okay otherwise.

"I did a double take," Mrs. Yuro-Clark, Sara's mom, says. "I wasn't sure if she had held her breath and made herself pass out, or what happened." Although she was familiar with epilepsy, it was the furthest thought from her mind.

Epilepsy is a brain disorder that causes the people who have it to experience recurring seizures. People with this illness don't look different from anyone else, and most of the time they feel normal. The problem comes during those times when the signals in their brains get mixed up. The result of this mix-up is a seizure.

Your brain controls everything. Things like sending signals to your hands and feet so you can wave hello and walk. It also controls the most basic things like your heartbeat and breathing. When everything is working the way it should, your brain keeps things in order. It communicates with the many parts of your body in perfect harmony. For some people, though, it's not that simple.

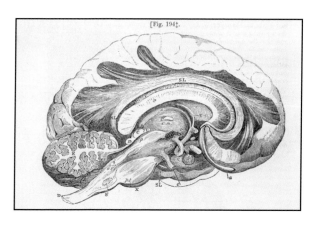

Above, a diagram of the human brain.

Imagine you are out on the basketball court and your coach starts calling out the play he wants you to run. Usually when the coach barks out the play, you and your teammates listen and then start running the play. Everyone works together to put the ball in the basket. The various parts of the team work together as one, and the entire process takes place because of clear communication. Your brain and body work together in much the same way. Your brain gives your body signals, and then your body acts them out.

Imagine that instead of hearing the play called from the coach, it sounds like he is yelling with his lips hot-glued together. And to make things even harder, he has also decided to try calling out the plays in a foreign language you don't understand. What would that look like? Well, it would be total chaos. This is very similar to what happens when a person's brain fails to clearly communicate with its body.

For epileptics, the electrical signals their brains send out can get mixed up. When this happens, these signals are not communicated correctly to their bodies. The brain is calling out instructions, but the body has no idea what the instructions mean. This is what a seizure is: total chaos.

What makes this disorder tough to deal with is that a seizure can come on at any moment, with no warning. Whether Sara is practicing her xylophone skills or playing a mean game of backgammon, the possibility of a seizure is always there.

Sara (right) and her sisters playing backgammon.

As a result of this, some epileptics try to keep their disorder hidden. Sometimes they even try to avoid social settings. The uncertainty of not knowing when a seizure will happen can keep an epileptic on edge. Epilepsy can be a very difficult disorder to deal with.

Many epileptics prefer to remain hidden from the world. Some are scared that their disorder will embarass them at the wrong moment.

Some people are embarrassed and secretive about their epilepsy. But there are many others who are open about it. After hopefully winning her first Academy Award, Sara won't be the only movie star to go public about having epilepsy. She will join other epileptic Hollywood actors like Danny Glover. Glover is most famous for his roles in the *Lethal Weapon* movies. Diagnosed with epilepsy as a teenager, Glover had seizures into his young adulthood. But they have subsided, and he is currently seizure free.

Unlike Danny Glover, actor Hugo Weaving still has seizures. Weaving is known for his roles as Agent Smith in *The Matrix* movies, and as Elrond in *The Lord of the Rings* trilogy. Weaving had his first seizure at thirteen and has been on medication to control them ever since. The threat of seizures is so great that he does not drive, afraid of losing control if a seizure were to come on while he was driving. Even a mild seizure like Sara's first one could have bad consequences on the road.

There are many other kinds of seizures, each with different symptoms. They can be mild like Sara's first one, with her eyes rolling back in her head and her losing consciousness for a few seconds. In some mild seizures, you don't even lose consciousness. Seizures like this involve only a small part of the brain.

But when the signals get really mixed up and the entire brain is involved, a seizure can get pretty nasty.

The worst kind of seizure is called a *generalized tonic-clonic seizure.* Someone having a seizure like this will lose consciousness and may even fall to the ground. At first, the body's muscles will tense up. Then there will be a period of fast muscle contractions that make the person's entire body shake uncontrollably. These seizures can last anywhere from a few seconds to several minutes. When the seizure is over, it usually takes some time for the person to recover. And they usually have no memory of anything out of the ordinary happening.

Most of the time, tonic-clonic seizures will end on their own. But in some severe cases the affected person may even stop breathing. This is when an ambulance should be called and medical attention is necessary. Without help, someone having these types of seizures is in serious danger.

Because of the violent movements during a tonic-clonic seizure, serious injuries can happen. If you have a seizure in an enclosed space, you could break a bone. Or you could even bite your tongue from the violent clenching of your jaw muscles.

After Sara's first seizure that summer afternoon, her mom called the doctor. Their doctor told her it was most likely an isolated incident that they would never see again. Single, isolated seizures in young children are not always a problem. And because it was so mild, Sara's doctor wasn't even sure that it was definitely a seizure.

But when almost the exact same thing happened again a month later, there was no denying there was a problem. Sara's parents got back on the phone with the doctor. He suggested tests to see what was going on. The tests didn't come soon enough, though. Sara's third seizure—"the big one"—as Sara's mom calls it, came before they got the chance to take any tests.

While her previous two episodes left Sara's parents wondering whether she had had a seizure, the third one left no doubt. When Sara's dad came home from work one September afternoon, Sara came rushing out of the house to greet him. But she never made it there. Still a few feet away from him, her legs gave out beneath her. Sara was having a full tonic-clonic seizure.

Sara lost consciousness and fell to the ground. Her arms straightened out violently and her fists clenched tightly. This gave way to the violent shaking and rapid muscle contractions that make a tonic-clonic seizure so scary.

The seizure did not end in a matter of seconds as her first two had. It seemed to go on endlessly. As the seizure continued, Sara eventually stopped breathing. Her tiny body continued to shake uncontrollably as her face turned dark red. Watching helplessly, Sara's parents called an ambulance.

The ambulance pulled up in a matter of minutes and the paramedics came running out. They put Sara onto a stretcher and into the ambulance. Once there, they managed to stabilize her and the seizure finally ended. To everyone's relief, she began breathing again.

At the hospital, the doctors watched Sara closely. They concluded that Sara was definitely having seizures, and from the looks of it they were only going to keep getting worse. The next step for the doctors was to figure out why Sara was having the mixed signals in her brain. And that meant they had to get *inside* her head.

Chapter Three

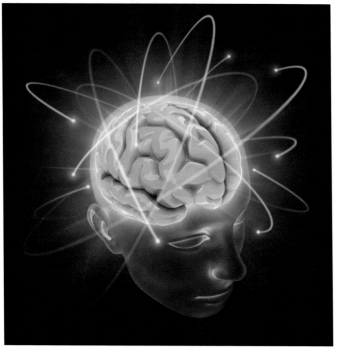

Brainpower

Your brain is an interesting organ if you stop to think about it for a moment. It's so interesting that Sara has decided if acting doesn't work out, she can become a neurologist (brain doctor) instead. It's always good to have a backup plan, and Sara likes to aim high.

Your brain can do things that are absolutely incredible. For example, try to remember what you had for breakfast this morning. Pretty easy, right? Now try to remember the name of your best friend when you were in second grade. A little bit harder, right? Now try remembering what you had for breakfast this morning while riding a bike and juggling. Okay, that might be a little much, but the point is still the same. Your brain is very good at doing many things at once.

In fact, at any given time, your brain is keeping millions of signals in order. It is making sure your heart keeps beating and your blood keeps pumping. These simple body functions don't just happen. Your brain is *making* them happen by constantly sending signals to your body. This happens even while you sleep. These signals tell your body to act, and it does.

A human brain weighs about three pounds. It feels as soft as an overripe avocado and has 100,000 miles of blood vessels feeding it. So although it fits neatly inside of your skull, if you were to take a look at your brain spread out, it would take up over three square feet of space.

People used to think that the bigger the brain, the smarter the person. For a long time, that logic was used to claim that men were smarter than women. This is because the average male brain is larger than the average female brain. Just try telling that to Albert Einstein, one of the smartest people in history. Mr. Einstein had a slightly smaller-than-average brain. Over time, it has been proven that brain size and intelligence in humans are not related.

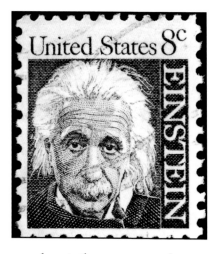

There is still a lot to learn about the power of our brains. In fact, most scientists would admit that we know very little about our brains. There are some scientists who think that if a person learned how to fully use their brain's power, they'd be able to do all sorts of amazing things. These things could include moving objects without touching them and seeing into the future.

Scientists in the 1970s studied a psychic named Felicia Parise. She insisted she could move things using only her mind. This is known as *telekinesis*. The scientists studying her placed several items under thick glass jars to make sure she couldn't touch them. They then watched in amazement as she made the items move without ever touching them. A pill box slid across the table several inches. A compass needle spun in circles, and pieces of aluminum foil floated around like they were flying.

When asked how she did it, Parise said that she concentrated very hard on the object and tried to develop a relationship with it. Once she had focused hard enough on the object, she would turn her muscular energy into mental energy. She would then use that force to move the object with her brain.

Apparently, it takes a lot of energy to move things with your mind because after this scientific study, Parise had lost a full two pounds and could barely move her arms. She gave up telekinesis after this experiment, saying it was too hard on her. Although it may have been a trick, the scientists studying her could never figure out how she was able to move those objects.

There are all kinds of unusual things that happen in our brains that point to how complex they are. For example, people with amputated limbs (meaning arms or legs that have been removed) have reported all sorts of strange things. Many claim that they wake up in the middle of the night and reach over to scratch an itch they feel on an arm that has not been there for years. These types of feelings in limbs that are no longer there are called phantom sensations.

Even if you haven't felt a phantom sensation, you have probably had your brain play a trick on you before. Have you ever been in a situation that you would swear you had experienced before? A strange feeling may have come over you that you had done that exact same thing some time in the past.

Don't worry, you are not going crazy! In fact, this happens to everyone from time to time. It's known as *déjà vu*, which means 'already seen' in French. Scientists can't seem to agree on an explanation for *déjà vu*. Some think it's a person remembering a very similar situation that may have occurred at some other point in their lives. Others think these moments are actually examples of the brain making a mistake, processing the experience as a memory before experiencing it as an event. And a handful of scientists think this feeling might be a look into our psychic abilities. These scientists believe that we can learn to use these abilities with the right training. *Déjà vu* is one mystery we may never be able to solve.

Because your brain is such a delicate organ, when doctors need to see inside it, they can't just open up your head and take a look. Instead, they slide you into a long tube called a magnetic resonance imaging machine, or an MRI.

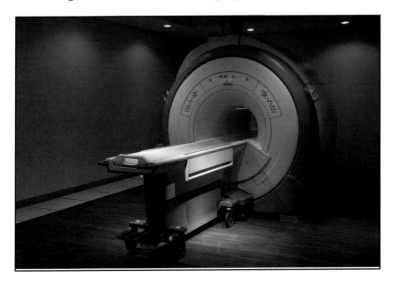

This machine can take a picture of the inside of your head without opening up your skull. It's similar to an x-ray, but it shows more than just your bones.

Because an MRI machine is basically a giant magnet, it's important for people to take off all their metal items before they're scanned. For people who have metal rods or plates in their bodies, an MRI is not an option. Doctors have to find other ways to get pictures of their insides.

After having several seizures at just two years old, Sara's doctors needed to see how her brain was working. Their hope was to slow down or get rid of her seizures. They put Sara into an MRI machine and started taking pictures of her brain.

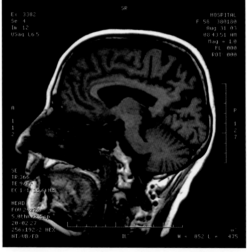

A real picture of the inside of someone's brain, taken by an MRI machine.

Though an MRI can take pictures of tumors and injuries, it's not the only way to see inside someone's head. Sara also had to be hooked up to an EEG (electroencephalograph). This test hooks a bunch of wires up to the outside of your head and measures your brain's electrical signals. That's right—brains actually produce electricity! Your brain's 100 billion neurons constantly send signals out to the rest of your body. In doing this, your brain makes enough electrical energy to run a twenty-five watt light bulb. With so many things to learn about brains, it's no wonder neurology is a close second to acting in Sara's list of career choices.

Sara's EEG test took place in the Epilepsy Monitoring Unit at a hospital close to her house. All the wires were hooked up to her head. The doctors watched over the signals her brain was sending out to her body. While Sara was hooked up to this EEG machine, her doctors looked for any signs of another seizure. They were hoping to be able to tell from where in her brain the miscommunications were coming. By doing this, they could begin to figure out the cause. But for this to happen, she needed to have a seizure while hooked up to the machine.

The doctors waited and waited. Sara's days in the Epilepsy Monitoring Unit passed slowly. She didn't have another seizure while being monitored. Eventually, the doctors unhooked her and sent her home. And although it wasn't an easy time for Sara, it wasn't entirely negative. To this day, Sara still has a strong interest in neurology and the human brain. She can trace this interest back to all her experiences with these tests and doctors.

After all the tests had been run, Sara's parents met with the doctor. The doctor delivered the news they had expected, but were still afraid to hear. "Your daughter has benign idiopathic epilepsy. She is having seizures, but we have not been able to locate their cause."

Chapter Four

Being Different

For several years after Sara's diagnosis, she would have multiple seizures a day. There was often no warning. Living with epilepsy was never easy, but Sara managed to have a pretty normal childhood. She never let epilepsy define her. Just like any other kid out there, she enjoyed doing typical kid stuff. She was just like everybody else.

Well, kind of…

Ask most kids about what kinds of pets they have, and the answers are pretty similar: a dog, a cat and maybe even some fish. But not Sara, who lives with a three-foot-long lizard named Jessica. Jessica gets to go for rides around the house on Sara's shoulder. In addition to Jessica, Sara has many other animals. She has two dogs, two cats, a bunch of fish and a guinea pig. But it doesn't end there. She also has two chinchillas, Winky and Hedwig.

Not very many people keep chinchillas - small South American rodents - as pets. In a way, Sara's taste for exotic animals makes a lot of sense. After all, actors are well known for being a weird bunch.

Rumor has it that for his role in *Charlie and the Chocolate Factory*, Johnny Depp wanted to be paid in red jelly beans instead of money. (Supposedly he was turned down because of tax reasons.) And Depp's co-star in *Pirates of the Caribbean,* Keira Knightley, reportedly wouldn't do the sequel to the movie unless the director promised her a sword fight in the film.

And then there's the prank Bill Murray supposedly pulled. Murray is famous for his roles in the *Ghostbusters* movies and *Caddyshack*. One New York City tourist tells the story of walking through a park when he felt someone's hands cover his eyes from behind and ask, "Guess who?" The tourist turned around, only to find famous actor Bill Murray staring back. Then Bill Murray supposedly said, "No one will ever believe you when you tell this story." And he walked away without another word.

As you can see, Sara should fit right in with a group of people so committed to being individuals. And Sara is definitely an individual. After all, how many *SpongeBob*-obsessed, iguana-loving actresses do you know?

Even though Sara has always done a great job of living life separate from her epilepsy, the disorder often finds a way to remind her that it's still there. Like one night in 1998 during a game of hide-and-go-seek with her two sisters. The youngest and smallest of the three, Sara had squeezed herself under her bed. She was convinced she had found the greatest hiding spot ever.

Once she got herself under there, however, she started having a seizure. This is dangerous enough on its own, but all the violent movements are even worse in a small space. Sara could have broken her bones or cracked her head open under there without quick action.

Machele ran off to get their parents. Kymmie dove under the bed to save Sara. Their parents showed up in the bedroom just as Kymmie was dragging Sara out from under the bed. The seizure finally stopped in the open safety of the bedroom. Sara escaped with no major injuries. Her sisters' quick thinking had saved the day.

As you can see, the physical aspects of epilepsy are very serious. But there is also another side of the disorder

Sara (center) and her sisters Machelle and Kymmie.

that isn't so easy for some to discuss. "Some people think just because you have epilepsy that means it's okay to act like a jerk around you," Sara says. "I know what it's like to be different. I know what it's like to be called names like 'Seizure Girl'. It hurts."

Kids can be pretty mean to each other. Unfortunately, being different often makes a young person a target for mean jokes. Sara has come across a few kids who have gone out of their way to be very cruel. Some of them have even gone as far as falling on the ground and shaking, trying to copy what it looks like when someone has a seizure.

"It doesn't make me angry when things like that happen, though," Sara says maturely. Then she adds with a smile, "Well, I guess that's not really true. There were a few kids who I definitely wanted to punch in the face." When she delivers this line, her sisters both begin laughing hysterically.

When the laughter quiets, Sara gets serious. "But I didn't punch them. The best way to deal with those kinds of people is to ignore them." Sara knows that people who are going to tease her are not worth getting worked up over.

Sara has done a bunch of research on the history of epilepsy. And she has been able to get a better understanding of the prejudice she often faced. She found out that the teasing she endured could have been a lot worse. And this is especially true if she had been born at another point in history.

For as long as people have known about epilepsy, it has often had a negative stigma. For hundreds of years, epileptics have suffered because of this. During ancient times, anyone who had seizures was thought to be possessed by demons. A witch-hunting handbook written in 1494 identifies a seizure as a "distinct sign of demonic possession." Having no way to understand the seizures, these early civilizations thought there was something evil about epileptics. They treated them harshly because of it. Epileptics were outcasts of societies who were often jailed and tortured. They were accused of being witches and even burned at the stake.

In the 1800s, people with seizures were often arrested and put in mental hospitals. People feared they were mentally ill and dangerous to others. Even as recently as one hundred years ago, it was illegal in some places for people with epilepsy to get married.

Although doctors understand epilepsy better now, there is still a negative stigma attached to it. Some ignorant people think epileptics are stupid, or crazy. But if you spent time chatting with Sara, you would know that none of these things are true. She reads books like she is a literature professor. And she has a huge vocabulary. She can also tell you all about the workings of the human brain. She's funny, outgoing and confident. Last but not least, she is an extremely talented actress.

Sara performing a song as "Annie" a few years back.

Despite scary moments like the seizure she had while underneath the bed, Sara keeps smiling. And it isn't always easy. After all, having epilepsy is not like having a cold. You don't just take some medicine and then sit in bed for a week, secretly hoping you never have to go back to school. In other words, it doesn't just clear up on its own.

And even after the seizures stop, an epileptic always lives in fear of the seizures coming back. This is something Sara lives with every day. Luckily, there are medications that can help correct the miscommunications happening in epileptics brains. But finding the right one is difficult.

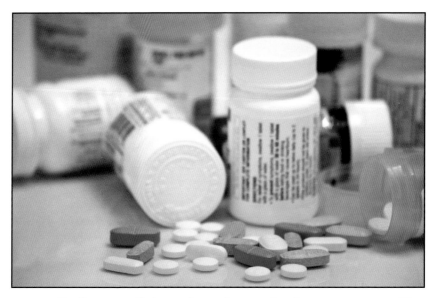

Sadly, medicine doesn't work for everyone. For these people, when all the other kinds of treatment fail, the last option is surgery. Although there are different kinds of surgical treatments, any kind of brain surgery is frightening. Before doctors can do any type of surgery, they must identify the part of the brain that is responsible for the miscommunications. This is not easy. To find out this information, doctors must actually see a patient having a seizure. And as Sara knows from experience, this is tricky.

If doctors can identify where the miscommunications are happening, they then have several options. The most serious surgery involves removing part of a person's brain.

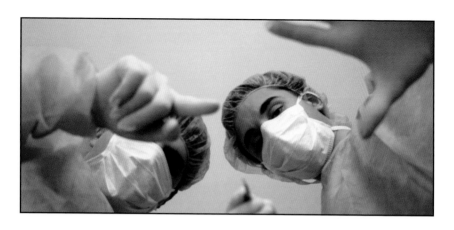

Having a piece of your brain removed sounds really painful, right? The strange truth is that the brain doesn't have any pain receptors. And it's not uncommon for patients to be awake during some brain surgeries. Although it seems like it would, brain surgery doesn't really hurt.

The really neat thing about this type of brain surgery is how the brain recovers. You would think that having a piece of your brain removed would change the way you remember, talk, etc…. But that's not usually the case. After the surgery, the remaining part of the brain learns to do all the things the removed part of the brain used to do. This is just another example of how amazing your brain is.

Sara was lucky enough to not have to go through any of that. Over time, her seizures began responding well to treatment. As the right combination of medication started to do its work, her seizures decreased. They didn't go away all at once, but they eventually stopped. The doctors could never explain what caused the seizures in the first place. And their disappearance was equally mysterious.

In 2001, Sara passed the two year mark without medication and still no seizures. The doctors declared that her seizures were most likely over. They had decreased Sara's medications a little bit at a time until she was completely off of them. They continued to keep an eye on her progress, and still do. The good news is that of the two million people in America with epilepsy, Sara is one of the few to get to this point. She is still off all medication and seizure free.

Today, Sara can often be found perfecting her back flips on the trampoline and hanging out with Jessica the iguana. Between that and her obsession with anything *SpongeBob* related, maybe she isn't exactly your *typical* teen. But she definitely has a good time being different.

Chapter Five

Nothing Is Impossible

So what's going on inside Sara's teenage brain today? Those who know Sara well might find the idea of seeing all the stuff she has going on up there frightening. But let's go ahead and take a look inside…

Wading through a pile of *SpongeBob* gear, we see that the inside of Sara's brain seems to be well organized. Digging deeper, we come across a poster of New York Mets' third baseman, David Wright. He is her favorite baseball player.

But don't tell this to Sara's mom, who is a lifelong Yankee fan! Moving further into her brain, we come across a drawer of Sara's memories. We see pictures of her Bat Mitzvah and her beloved grandmother.

Finally, we find the memory of one of the most important nights of Sara's life. It's the memory of the time her parents took the family to Broadway to see *Mamma Mia.* They even got the chance to meet all the actors in the show.

It was Memorial Day 2006, and eleven-year-old Sara waited near the stage after the show had ended. She had heard that the actors would come out and talk to the crowd. Just about everyone else had left when the actors came out. Everything worked out perfectly, and Sara and her family had the cast to themselves. The same actors who were up on the stage earlier were now standing right in front of her.

Sara listened to the cast talk about the show. It was then she decided there was nothing she wanted to do more than be an actress. When times are tough for Sara, she often returns to this memory. She uses it as motivation to keep moving forward.

With her seizures behind her, Sara's attention turned to the stage. In the summer of 2007, Sara landed her next role. It was in a community theater production. And it took on a really special meaning for her.

The play, *Up the Peastalk*, was a bit strange, but the audience seemed to really enjoy it. How strange? Well, at one point, there was a cow carrying two toilet plungers across the stage, and a little yellow bird marching through the crowd chanting: "Nothing is impossible." There was also a singing bush and a man with one huge foot.

The cast of Up the Peastalk poses for a picture.

It wasn't Sara's first chance to play a non-human character that made this performance so special (she played the yellow bird). The play meant so much to her because of its theme: Nothing is impossible. Thinking about everything she had overcome, Sara appreciated the power of those words. While getting ready to make her first entrance, Sara got into character by repeating the words "nothing is impossible".

When actors *get into character,* it means they are trying to become the character they're playing. There are all kinds of things Sara has to consider about a character. She considers things like what kind of a personality her character has, and what its voice sounds like.

There are a few famous movie actors who take this process so seriously that they'll stay in character for days at a time. Even when they aren't performing, they'll make people call them by their characters' names. Actor Will Ferrell has made an art of this. While doing a publicity tour for the movie *Anchorman,* he did interviews as his character. He insisted that everyone call him either Ron or Mr. Burgundy, his character's name.

In the community theater play, Sara was faced with the difficulty of playing a character that wasn't even human.

The Wandering Warbler was a singing bird who guides the rest of the characters on a quest. Sara's sisters will jokingly tell you that playing an animal isn't that big a stretch for her. But Sara still had to get the audience to believe she was really a bird.

Flapping her yellow wings and singing all of her lines, Sara really became her character. Even when she wasn't directly involved in the action on the stage, she would move her feathers and wings like a bird.

Wanting to be a part of every aspect of creating her character, Sara helped a family friend make her costume. They made a set of wings and a tail. Combined with her bird-like movements, Sara transformed herself into that little yellow bird. The performance was a great success. Sara loved acting like a bird, and she really enjoyed creating the costume. After all, costume design and special effects are both things Sara's interested in.

The play didn't have the same kind of special effects like movies such as *I, Robot*, Sara's favorite movie. But it was convincing for a stage production of a fairy tale.

Besides, great acting always beats out special effects. Many of the movies we watch today are filled with tricks. We are definitely entertained by large explosions and realistic-looking monsters. However, the movies we remember are the ones with the best plots and good acting. The special effects are like icing on the cake.

However, Hollywood special effects weren't always so special. In the early days, special effects were pretty basic. *The War of the Worlds*, before it was a Tom Cruise movie, was a radio play. It was broadcast on the night before Halloween in 1938. It is a great example of how far special effects have come.

Before televisions were a common part of every household, people listened to the radio. Radio plays were the old-fashioned version of today's television shows. Believe it or not, people would tune in every week for their favorite programs.

An old fashioned radio.

The War of the Worlds was one of these old radio plays about an alien invasion. And it took an interesting approach to special effects.

During *The War of the Worlds* broadcast, a newscaster was describing an invading alien ship. The audience could hear the craft making an eerie sound in the background. "The doors are beginning to open now," the nervous voice cracked. The creepy sound in the background got louder. But in fact, the sound the audience was listening to wasn't a spaceship's door opening at all.

In that radio studio, a member of the sound crew had recorded himself doing something bizarre. He had been unscrewing the lid of a peanut butter jar inside a toilet bowl. This made an echoing sound. The audience thought they had been listening to the alien ship landing and its doors beginning to open. But they were actually hearing a peanut butter jar being unscrewed in a  toilet. Not exactly the kind of high-tech effects you'd expect today!

No one could have possibly believed the sound was the opening of a UFO's doors, right? Wrong. The broadcast of *The War of the Worlds* seemed so realistic that many people thought the play was an actual news broadcast!

Despite repeated warnings that the program was entirely fictional, many people called the police in a panic. Some even claimed to be able to smell the poison gas used by the invading aliens. There were even some people who heard the broadcast who took to the street, ready to defend themselves. So, although the special effects were primitive, they were definitely believable enough. Still, it's nothing like movies nowadays.

Today, characters can perform slow-motion martial arts and appear to float. Exploding cars can jump over lanes of traffic. It's a far cry from a peanut butter jar in a toilet. And who knows what kinds of new technology will be available for movies in the future.

The special effects you see today have been made possible by advances in computer-generated imagery, or CGI. What you see up on the screen in those special effects scenes is actually just a picture created by a computer. The rampaging T-Rex in *Jurassic Park* was nothing more than an image created by a graphic artist on a computer. It was then inserted into the film.

In the early days of movies, this effect probably would have been made by putting an actor inside a bad dinosaur costume. He would then trample his way through a small set to make him look huge. The old *Godzilla* movies are full of these types of effects.

When watching an old horror movie, you might find yourself laughing instead of being scared. Sara thinks that Jason from the original *Friday the 13th* is absolutely hilarious. But the scary girl from *The Ring* keeps her up at night.

Working on the stage most of the time, Sara hasn't had the pleasure of working with snarling monsters or giant lizards. But with a little luck that could all change. Despite all her success on the stage, Sara wants to branch out into screen acting.

With a movie audition under her belt, Sara recently got the chance to be in a short commercial. It was about a young adult book called *The Garden of Eve*. Sara thought that filming the commercial was a blast! And it was also a great learning experience.

Being Sara.

Although her acting career was beginning to take off, there was something else Sara felt she needed to get involved in.

Chapter Six

Getting Involved

Rising above your difficulties and being able to put them behind you is a great thing. However, it's also important to never forget your past. When you remember the tough times, you are more likely to be willing to help those who are still struggling.

Whether she gets the part in the *American Girl* movie or not, Sara never wants to forget her difficult battle with epilepsy. Her quest to remember was how "Sara's Walk for Epilepsy" was born.

Sara is part of a long tradition of successful people who want to give back to their communities. Dwayne Wade is one of the greatest basketball players in the world. But he wasn't always a millionaire superstar. He was able to make it through a tough childhood in the south side of Chicago.

In 2003, Wade founded The Wade's World Foundation in an effort to give something back. His organization helps fund education, health, and social skills for at-risk kids growing up in urban areas. Since making it to the NBA, D-Wade has donated millions of dollars of his own money. Sure, he makes a ton of money, but that just means he can give more back to the community.

With this same kind of generosity in mind, Sara wanted to do something to get involved in her community and help those who still struggle with seizures like she did. And since she didn't have millions of dollars, she decided the best way to help was by donating her time.

One afternoon, her mother was on her way to a charity fund drive. The event was a walk organized to raise money for breast cancer. The money would go towards research and awareness. Sara's mom had gone to several charity events that year. She had also helped raised money for heart disease and autism.

Seeing how all of these events were so helpful, Sara got to thinking. "Mom," she said, after she had returned from her walk to support breast cancer. "I see all these events for all these causes. How come there is never an event for epilepsy?"

The question was completely valid. It almost seemed as though fundraising for epilepsy had been forgotten. Without funding, scientists don't have as many resources for research. Events like charity walks help raise money and awareness. They can be the driving forces behind curing diseases.

A few hours after their conversation, Sara had a plan for her own event. She was going to have a charity epilepsy walk through the New Paltz college campus. She contacted the local Epilepsy Foundation that afternoon and told them all about her idea. The goal was to raise money for epilepsy research and awareness. She also wanted to help break the negative stigma the disorder has.

This was a difficult project for anyone to organize, but especially so for a teenager. The people at the Foundation were skeptical at first. They didn't want Sara to get her hopes up. Although they were happy to offer support, they were cautious. "Maybe you'll raise five hundred dollars," they said. "If you write up a proposal, we'll take a look at it."

Sara got the plan on paper and brought it to the Epilepsy Foundation. They were still unsure of how such a big event could be pulled together by someone so young. But they continued to work with her anyway. They told Sara that if she could find a place to hold the event, then she could go ahead with it with their full support.

Next, Sara went to the office of the president of the college in her town. There was a street on campus Sara thought would be the perfect place for her walk. All she needed was permission to use the college campus for her event. And then everything would fall into place.

Sara confidently walked into the conference room. She had the proposal and a dream of educating those in her community about epilepsy. She took a seat at the head of a long table.

A few minutes later, the president walked in. He looked puzzled by the presence of a young girl sitting in *his* chair. He glanced at her for a moment, and then sat in a smaller chair to her left. Several other people walked into the room and the meeting began.

Sara read her proposal. She explained her vision to the room full of adults. When she finished her presentation, she turned to the president and said, "So you're going to help me, right?" Sara was unwilling to take no for an answer.

"Absolutely," he responded, realizing Sara would not

be denied.

That same day, Sara and her family went to work. They made preparations for "Sara's Walk for Epilepsy." They made flyers to stick around town. They also recorded a few commercials to play on the local radio stations. These really helped draw attention to the event. Then they planned a two-mile walking route. The route went around the college campus. They found walkers and sponsors to raise money. They got local businesses to donate items to be used as raffle prizes. And they designed t-shirts and bracelets to give away. It was a lot of work, but the months of planning flew by. Then, one sunny April morning, the big day arrived.

Early in the morning the main square on the college campus looked like a rock concert. Everyone was packed around a small podium. Many people were wearing blue "Sara's

Walk for Epilepsy" bracelets and t-shirts. Volunteers, friends and family members had all come out to support Sara and epilepsy. There were hundreds of attendees.

After welcoming everyone, Sara's dad introduced her. Sara had thought for a week about what she was going to say at this moment. The setting was perfect. She hopped up on a stop sign to get a better look at the community she had brought together. The crowd hushed, awaiting her words.

A few minutes earlier Sara had realized that the speech she had prepared was no longer in the pocket of her pants. Maybe it had fallen out while she was stuffing her dachshund, Cooper, into a "Sara's Walk" t-shirt. The crowd began to stir and she knew she had to say *something...anything*.

Being a skilled actress, she didn't panic. Instead, she improvised. Even though Sara "ran out of words," she kept her cool. She opened "Sara's Walk for Epilepsy" like a pro. When her speech ended, the entire crowd cheered and yelled. And then the walk started with a bang.

The next few hours were awesome. Hundreds of walkers made their way around the two-mile route. It seemed more like a big party than a charity event. The adults all stuck together and made their way slowly around the course. The young people were a different story. They were joking around the whole time and having a blast. Sara and her friends were definitely running the show.

They couldn't have asked for a better day than that April morning. It was sunny and warm—even a little hot. At one point, things got pretty crazy with all the water bottles everyone had. It started out as a joke. Sara and her sisters innocently squirted some of their friends with water. The next thing Sara knew, people were soaking each other and emptying their water bottles onto their friends' heads. The walk turned into an all-out water fight. Everyone who was there agrees that it was a great time.

The walkers made their way back to the beginning of the route. And that's where the party really got started. There were all kinds of food, games, a d.j. and dancing. It was a huge outdoor party with the whole community involved. The prizes that had been donated by local businesses were raffled off. The party lasted well into the afternoon.

In the middle of all the festivities, Sara's parents handed her an envelope. She wondered what in the world it could be. Sara gave it a little shake before opening it. And then she carefully opened it. Inside was a beautiful piece of United States Senate letterhead. Sara noticed her own name on top of the letter and skimmed quickly down to the end. She saw a handwritten signature at the bottom of the letter. It read: Hillary Rodham Clinton, United States Senator.

All of Sara's charity work had caught the attention of the former First Lady. She had written Sara a personal letter of thanks. Sara felt great pride as she read Senator Clinton's words: "Your inspiring example and determination demonstrate how a single individual can make a remarkable difference in the lives of others."

When everyone had gone home for the night, Sara and her family were amazed by the results. They had raised over $15,000 for epilepsy in just that one day! Not bad when you consider she was told she would be lucky to raise even five hundred dollars.

They had so much success that afternoon that "Sara's Walk for Epilepsy" has become an annual event. Sara has raised over $40,000 for epilepsy. More importantly, Sara has proved that those with epilepsy can do anything they set their minds to. And this goes a long way toward breaking the stigma associated with the disorder.

Chapter Seven

Looking Forward

After her successful charity event, Sara thought about what to do next. Her hope was to find a way to bring together two of her passions: acting and epilepsy advocacy. Once again, the local Epilepsy Foundation provided all the support she could have asked for. The Foundation designed an ad campaign to help continue educating people about epilepsy.

The campaign started out pretty small. Sara first appeared on posters. They went up on buses, trains and taxis throughout New York. "We are your friends, your neighbors, your co-workers," the bottom of the posters read. It drove home the point that people with epilepsy lead perfectly normal lives and are no different from anybody else.

Sara remembers the first time she saw one of the posters. On a long bus ride home from a school field trip, she glanced out the window. Posted on the side of an Albany city bus, the ad jumped out at her. She was staring herself in the face through the window. The rest of the kids on the bus climbed over each other to get a look at her ad. She felt really proud and excited. It was another great moment for Sara.

These posters were just the beginning. Sara's face eventually found its way onto huge billboards, too.

Sara, far left, on a billboard in upstate New York.

While driving, Sara and her family often ran into these giant pictures of her. The coolest part of the ad campaign was when the campaign organizers decided to do television commercials. This was when Sara finally made the leap from the stage to the screen.

The director of the commercial didn't share Sara's excitement about the project at first. When told he would be working with a teenager, he was a little worried. Would she be good in front of the camera? Would she be able to deliver the lines without messing up? Would she even show up on time?

Of course, Sara did make it to the studio right on time. When she got there, a production assistant handed her some cue cards. The plan was for Sara to read the lines as they filmed her. Smiling up at the director a few moments later, Sara politely told him that she didn't need the cue cards. She had already memorized her lines and was ready to get started.

"Okay," the director said, smiling, "Sara is ready to go. So let's roll!"

Take one is usually just for practice. Directors and actors use it as a way of making sure that everything is in order. So when the camera started rolling for take one, the director didn't expect much. He called action, giving Sara the cue to begin her lines. She got through them like a pro. She didn't stammer, and she did it with great emotion.

"She's a natural," the director remarked. Then he walked over to Sara and said, "We can probably use that one. But let's do a couple more takes just to see what you can do, okay?"

The next few takes went smoothly. Sara improvised a bit as she grew more confident. In adding her own touch to the part she made it uniquely her own.

Making it look easy, Sara finished the commercial shoot. It was edited and released. It found its way onto local stations and eventually onto some major networks all over New York. Sara's message spread quickly, helping to educate her community. It even made her a local celebrity. Sara was recognized all over town by people who had seen her billboards and commercials.

In the same way that her trip to Broadway to see *Mamma Mia* inspired Sara, having such a great time doing this commercial cemented her dream. Some day, she would become a famous movie actress.

A few months later Sara saw the ad for the open casting call for the *American Girl* movie. She had no doubt she would be there. The billboards and TV commercials had gotten her some recognition. She could only imagine what would happen if she actually got the part in a Hollywood film.

The day of the audition was long and stressful. But it

was definitely a lot of fun too. After all, Sara was sitting in a waiting room, ready to be called in for the second round of auditions. She tapped her foot anxiously, clutching her ticket into the second audition. There were many talented girls surrounding her. Making the first cut had really built up Sara's confidence.

Without looking, Sara reached her hand down the leg of the chair she was sitting in. She felt for the initials S.C. she had etched into the chair earlier. She ran her fingers over the names and initials of all the other girls. She stopped when she came to her own. Sara felt like she had already accomplished so much, whether she got the part or not.

The remaining girls continued to enter the auditorium for their first audition. Some of them came out waving numbers excitedly. However, most just grabbed their things and headed for the door. The line outside got shorter. Finally, just the girls who were called back for round two were left. There were about fifty girls left in total.

The room was quieter than it was before, but no less intense. Sara studied her script. She waited for her group to be called in for the second reading. At last she heard her group called. Sara attached the number 116 proudly to the front of her shirt. She found her spot on the blue-tape line again.

"Get your toes right on that line, girls. Otherwise you might get eaten by the sharks we keep under the stage," a member of the casting team called out. He was trying to keep everyone from getting too nervous. It was a pretty lame joke, but Sara smiled anyway.

The audition started again just like it did the first time. One after the other, the girls in front of Sara said their names and read their lines. This time, however, a man with a movie camera followed the whole thing. As each girl spoke, the camera zoomed in tight on her.

Listening to the other girls, it sounded like a room full of professional actresses. Each line was delivered with emotion and accuracy. The girls seemed to transform themselves into their characters. They were brilliant. Sara knew that the great ones always raise their game in big moments. The great ones give their best performance when the pressure is highest.

The camera moved down the line and came to a stop in front of Sara. The red recording light snapped on. It was time. The camera felt like it was two inches in front of her face. Sara looked up, smiled like it wasn't even there, and went right into her lines.

"My name is Sara-Elizabeth…."

The lines were the same as they were in the first audition, but the performance wasn't. It was better. Her timing was dead on. Her voice changed from her own. It really captured her character's feelings. Without even thinking about it, she dropped her script mid-delivery to move her hands just like her character would. The casting directors watched and smiled as Sara became the character she was reading for.

She finished her lines, then paused a moment. She bent down to pick up the script she had dropped. She caught a glimpse of the number 116 on her shirt as she straightened back up. The cameraman quickly moved to the next girl in line. It was the shortest performance of her lifetime. Still, it was among the most satisfying performances of her short career. She stood proudly and listened as the other girls read their lines.

"Thank you very much, girls. We've got a tough decision to make here. You all did such a great job. You'll hear from us in a couple of weeks," one of the casting directors said as she walked out with the group.

Walking into the second audition, Sara's main concern had been landing the part. On her way out, though, that changed. She knew that whether she got the part or not wasn't really all that important. Performing well under the pressure of that audition was a huge step forward. It was a step in making her red carpet dreams come true. Surrounded by so many other young actresses, she had given her best performance ever. And Sara had overcome so much just to show up at the audition.

Sara and her dad headed out into the New York City evening among the crowd of teenage actresses. They were all tired after a long day. They prepared to cross the busy street and make their way back home.

Just then, a city bus noisily pulled up to let off some passengers. Surrounded by the group of actresses, Sara stood staring at one of her Epilepsy Foundation ads. It was plastered to the side of the bus. A few girls did a double take at the poster and then back at Sara. But she wasn't sure if anyone really connected the dots. Either way, it was a really cool moment. It was as if both of her worlds had come together.

The bus disappeared into the heavy New York traffic.

In Sara's mind, it magically transformed into that same zebra-striped Hummer limousine she had imagined earlier. Sara followed it in her mind as it cruised up Broadway and into the city's theater district. It went past where *Mamma Mia* was outside the Winter Garden Theatre.

Sara joined her father in the car for the ride back home. She thought about her past and all she had gone through to get where she was. She let out a long and satisfied sigh. She reflected on what had been quite an amazing journey. Sara can only imagine what the future has in store. She knows that the possibilities are as limitless as the amazing world she has inside her own head.

Want more Sara?

www.itsnotwhoiam.com